The Love Affair Continues

From Manhattan
to Mississippi

Part Two

The Love Affair Continues

From Manhattan to Mississippi

Part Two

Daisy Karam-Read

QUAIL RIDGE PRESS
BRANDON, MISSISSIPPI

ISBN-13: 978-1-934193-50-1 • ISBN-10: 1-934193-50-X

Printed in Canada

Cover and chapter-opening illustrations by

Liquid
CREATIVE
www.liquid-creative.com

Design by Cyndi Clark

Library of Congress Cataloging-in-Publication Data

Karam-Read, Daisy.
   The love affair continues : From Manhattan to Mississippi, part two / Daisy Karam-Read.—1st ed.
   p. cm.
   Continues: From Manhattan to Mississippi. Brandon, Miss. : Quail Ridge Press, c2007.
   ISBN-13: 978-1-934193-50-1
   ISBN-10: 1-934193-50-X
1. Mississippi--Social life and customs. 2. Ocean Springs (Miss.)—Social life and customs.
3. Southern States—Social life and customs. 4. North and south. 5. Karam-Read, Daisy.
6. Ocean Springs (Miss.)—Biography. 7. Manhattan (New York, N.Y.)—Biography. 8. New York
(N.Y.)—Biography. I. Karam-Read, Daisy. From Manhattan to Mississippi. II. Title.
III. Title: From Manhattan to Mississippi, part two.
   F345.K375 2010
   976.2—dc22   2010030636

First edition

QUAIL RIDGE PRESS
P. O. Box 123 • Brandon, Mississippi 39043
1-800-343-1583 • www.quailridge.com

In memory of my aunt,
Hélène Karam,
a painter in Paris

Contents

Preface

IT WAS A GRAY AND DRIZZLY DAY in Vicksburg, but I was glad to be at Lorelei Books signing my first book, *From Manhattan to Mississippi*. A man approached me, introduced himself as Milton M., and complimented me. "I enjoyed your book and I'm glad that you like the people of Mississippi," he said. "But the Gulf Coast isn't really Mississippi. And you've spent entirely too much time in New Orleans."

He grew up in Smith County and still owns a house there. The nearest neighbor is two miles down the road, the nearest Wal-Mart and McDonald's, twenty miles away. For company, a cow might occasionally come to visit. Although he now lives in Vicksburg, Milton said that if I wanted to understand Mississippi, I should live in Smith County and write about that. "Spend a year or eighteen months there, and you'll know Mississippi."

Well, that kind of isolation is too much for me. Aside from not wanting to leave my husband for a year, I knew that as a former New Yorker accustomed to living with neighbors on all sides, I'd be terrified of living alone out in the country. But I knew he was right. It's been twelve years since I fell in love with a

Mississippi man and left Manhattan for a new life with him on the Mississippi Gulf Coast. In my first book I described my joy over discovering the friendly people and their artistic sensibilities, the distinctive food, and the scenic, historic places on the Coast. And now I've come to realize that the Coast is not, in all ways, typical of the Magnolia State. Yes, the people are great everywhere—we have friends throughout the state—yet each region of Mississippi has its own distinct character.

So I didn't go to live in Smith County or in any other part of Mississippi. I remained on the Coast. In the last two and one-half years, however, I've crisscrossed the highways and back roads of the state, thanks to a lively schedule of book signings. My travels have been glorious. I was already acquainted with Jackson and Oxford, but I discovered Poplarville, Hattiesburg, Bruce, Natchez, Flowood, Tupelo, Picayune, Greenwood, Rolling Fork, Ridgeland, Clarksdale, Cleveland, and so many other places. I loved each one of them, and I loved the stories the people who lived there told me. Everywhere, the people of Mississippi have stories.

Mississippians from the Delta insist that Coast inhabitants are different, and the Gulf Coast citizens swear that other Mississippians look at things in a completely different way. Both are right, of course, to a degree. The land itself accounts for many of the differences, as geography has shaped the lives of the people over generations. But I've found that more things bind Mississippians together than set them apart.

Accents vary. Delta people pronounce many words uniquely. When I first moved to the South, Jerry introduced me to chic Scottie Webster, originally from Greenville, now residing in New Orleans. She spoke of a "Chiyuh" and I had no idea what she was talking about. Was she referring to Chai, the popular tea of India and South Asia? I remained mystified and silent, but as the conversation progressed, I realized that she had said "chair."

Pronunciation aside, almost everyone uses the same expressions throughout Mississippi. Some phrases are chivalrous. I've heard southern men introduce their wives as "my bride," only to learn that they had been married thirty years. And the first time Jerry uttered the phrase, "That dog won't hunt," I was baffled. "What dog?" I asked. And when a southerner tells me a place is "over yonder," I'm still uncertain where "yonder" actually is. A Mississippi lady recently explained it: "Over yonder is where you're not." Oh.

And there's that wonderful word "caddywampus." When something is caddywampus, it's askew. Apparently, the word originated in the Tennessee and Kentucky hills and refers to a wildcat. The fast running wildcat, frequently frightened by humans, runs with its back legs very off center, which makes him look misaligned, or catawampus.

IN THE PAGES THAT FOLLOW, I write mostly about Mississippi, but I also touch on Louisiana and Alabama, because these neighboring states continue to be a vital part of my southern education. As different as these states are from one another, they share characteristics that clearly distinguish them from the rest of the United States. With each year, I've gained increased respect for the people of the Deep South. I've met many successful people, most of whom started out with very little. More than in most other regions of our country, they've had an economic struggle. And they've triumphed brilliantly. Genius knows no geographical boundaries.

Surely their stories, and others like them, are the true songs of the South.

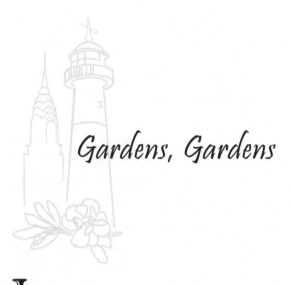

Gardens, Gardens

IT COULD BE GIVERNY. As I watch my neighbor Pat West tending her garden in the early morning hours, I think of Claude Monet, the Impressionist painter, and his beloved garden in France. Pat has neither a Japanese bridge nor a lily pond, but the care she puts into growing things on Wanda Place evokes Monet's passion for his Giverny. With her garden shears in hand and a straw hat shielding her head, Pat looks serene in the diffused light, pruning her roses before the sun's glare overtakes the day.

Because she has created her picturesque garden, I enjoy my view as I walk out to get the newspaper. Before I read the dire headlines, I take a moment to look at her yard across the street. I love the old-fashioned lamppost and the two planters on either side of the path to her front door. They're filled with snapdragons and white, pale yellow, and purple tulips, their heads trembling in the morning breeze. Spring is just a week away as I write this, and oh, the marvel of spring in Mississippi. Nearby are pale pink azaleas, a splash of fuchsia at their center. Wind chimes sound softly. A birdbath stands in the middle of the lawn. An American flag next to Pat's door stirs in the morning air. I take it all in. It's a beautiful composition.

Watching over it all is a statue of St. Francis. I remember how Pat's puppy, B.G., barked furiously at the statue. Pat explained to her dog, "That's St. Francis, B.G." Unappeased, her tirade at this still and silent stranger continued. Pat repeated, "That's St. Francis, the patron saint of animals." But B.G. was intractable. The little mutt, who has the soft mouth of a retriever and the lung capacity of a runner, was insistent upon protecting Pat from this trespassing saint. B.G.'s origins are unknown to Pat, but she says, "I'm sure her mother comes from a long line of proper southern ladies, and she had a brief, but memorable encounter with a traveling man."

Pat is a Mississippian by choice—and now a diehard. When she speaks of her late father, she says, "My daddy"—the indisputable mark of a southern woman. If you hear a northern woman who is past the age of childhood saying "Daddy," you can be sure she means an entirely different kind of daddy. Pat was born in Ohio and lived in Mississippi between the ages of five and six. Growing up, she lived in several other places, and returned to attend the University of Southern Mississippi. Pat has stayed in her home and waited out every single hurricane over the last forty years.

GO TO ANY NEWSSTAND and look at the national women's interest magazines. You'll see an abundance of articles on how to get organized, boost your memory, reinvent your career, and make dinner faster; how to dress with confidence and pare down your beauty routine; how to improve your relationships, protect your investment portfolio, and save on home repairs. Now pick up a southern women's interest magazine. In addition to the usual self-improvement pieces, you'll find a wealth of articles on landscaping and gardens—winter gardens, container gardens, and community gardens; on making topiaries and flowerbeds, arranging flowers in your home, and, for the beginning gardener, planting your first bulbs. There's garden inspiration for everyone.

I don't know any suburban New York women who belong to a garden club. I'm sure they must exist, but I've never met them. And for all of us living in the city who yearned for verdant beauty, the answer was always the same: "You want green? Go to Central Park." If we were lucky enough to have a terrace, we put a flowerpot out there and let the rain do the rest. When I had my first apartment in Manhattan, a friend gave me a dieffenbachia plant. I appreciated it because it required so little care. But then I heard that it was poisonous. Since I had a stray kitten up for adoption I banished the plant. That sums up my horticultural experience.

In Los Angeles the scenario was the same. Southern California is beautiful, with sunshine and flowers everywhere. Although it's a semi-desert, everything blooms. But I've never met a lady there who belongs to a garden club. And I've never seen a woman dig in her garden. Excellent professional gardeners come in bi-monthly or bi-weekly to maintain the lawns.

But many southern women put their hands into the earth. Southerners seem to connect with nature intimately and have a deep love for their gardens. Mississippians—men and women—listen to popular statewide radio shows devoted to plants and gardening, mostly flowers and shrubs, but vegetables, too. Mississippi newspapers overflow with columns and articles on the subject. Southerners don't just enjoy their gardens as most Americans do; they celebrate their gardens.

"Does your magnolia molt? Do your daylilies droop? Did you buy blueberry plants at the Red, White & Blueberry Festival and are stuck with what to do with them?" These questions came to me in an email from the Oceans Springs Chamber of Commerce. But help was at hand! Dr. Gary R. Bachman, I was assured, would be at the Ocean Springs Fresh Market to answer these vexing questions.

My future husband Jerry arrived at my door for our first date in Manhattan, bowed, and presented me with camellias from his garden in Ocean Springs. He had picked those delicate flowers that morning and carried them onto the plane, and that touched me deeply. Even with my lack of gardening knowledge, I was impressed. How much more personal this was than buying a bouquet.

ALTHOUGH JULY IS THE HOTTEST MONTH in south Mississippi, the summer heat lingers into September and October. That difficult post-Hurricane Katrina autumn of 2005 seemed unseasonably warm. Our home had been destroyed, and I was digging in the debris on our property, hoping to find something—anything—when I suddenly realized that I was sweltering because most of our trees were gone and along with them, their shade. I hadn't appreciated the trees' protectiveness before. Stripped of so many trees after the hurricane, the Mississippi Gulf Coast was desolate.

There was so much to do, so many necessary, critical undertakings—mourn those who had died, tend to those who became ill after the storm, rebuild bridges and businesses and homes, buy furniture when a house was finally ready—that we didn't immediately try to bring back the natural beauty. But before long our citizens started thinking of ways to recapture nature's gifts. In January 2007, sixteen months after the catastrophe, the Mississippi Department of Transportation crews began removing dead trees from the medians of U.S. Highway 90, locally known as Beach Boulevard because it skirts the Gulf of Mexico nearly all the way across Mississippi.

Before Katrina ravaged the Coast, a grand procession of venerable live oak trees had graced these center medians, many of them estimated to be five or six hundred years old. Their magnificent beauty highlighted my daily drives down the thoroughfare. But the rush of saltwater during the storm attacked them at their roots, and after the hurricane, lifeless tree trunks remained.

The first person to rescue us from the depressing sight was Marlin Miller, a wood sculptor from Ft. Walton Beach, Florida. He offered his time and talent—gratis—to transform a few remnants into sculptures, and he worked assiduously. At first, I could hardly imagine art emerging from these remains. Daily, we watched as Miller slowly brought shape and life to the stumps, using a variety of steel chain saws, and refining his work with grinders, sanders, and chisels. Finally, the metamorphosis was complete. The tree trunks of dozens of once live oaks had been reincarnated into works of art, dotting the barren medians with seagulls, seahorses, dolphins, and herons. Later, Mississippi native and award-winning chainsaw artist/wood-carver Dayton Scoggins, created additional sculptural works in Biloxi. All stand testament to the Coast's connection to local marine life and to the resilience of our people.

Residents of neighborhoods and communities have worked together in ways large and small to bring back the once exquisite Coastal region. About twenty of us who live in the Broadmoor Place Subdivision in Gulfport gathered at Pat's house, ready to organize a task force to beautify our neighborhood. "If you restore the beauty of the earth, you restore the beauty of the people who live on it," our organizer Martha Boyce said. Our goal was to plant the "neutral grounds" (an expression I'd never heard until I moved to the South) along our area streets. The neutral grounds are small plots, a chance mixture of vegetation, deeded to the public in the original subdivision. We were gathered to formulate a plan for planting and maintaining them. Before this meeting, no one was accountable for these little parcels of land. So there I was in mid-March, among these garden-loving neighbors (eighteen women, two men) with a goal: to beautify these green spaces.

Ms. Boyce's plans for neighborhood beautification were ambitious. "We have to reconnect to the beauty of our southern environment," she said. Her vision was big, but her esthetic desire was rooted in practicality. "First, we'll have to clean up all the triangles," she continued. "Someone will have to turn on the water. I'm not a gardener," she admitted, "but I'll try to get money; I'll try to get support. What we have now is a foundation, a 501 C-3. All services are donated. We're not paying anyone." Her enthusiasm was contagious; the shared love of nature unified our community. "The Mississippi Gulf Coast can do anything," Martha said. "My granddaughter is going to walk in beauty."

As she spoke, I was reminded of the lovely vest-pocket parks scattered throughout New York City. Like our neutral grounds, vest pocket parks are tiny, but what a welcome respite from the clamor of Manhattan! Since our meeting the city of Gulfport has planted two of the neutral grounds with easy-to-care-for plants. But the city ran out of funds, and neighborhood garden-lovers like ours have been holding garage sales to raise money to purchase ground cover and azaleas. A sense of community and a love of growing things can work wonders.

IT WAS TWILIGHT NOW. Back home after a day's work, Pat was enjoying her garden. She would be able to linger there only a little while before the gnats and mosquitoes found her. She sat a few minutes on a bench petting Mitzi, one of her Maine Coon cats. A white dogwood tree in full bloom was their umbrella. I gazed as the sky turned deep purple and she walked from her garden into her amber-lit house.

Saturday Mornings

"**S**UMMER AFTERNOON – summer afternoon . . . the two most beautiful words in the English language," wrote Henry James.

I picture James in a white linen suit, sitting in a sunlit English garden. He is sipping a Pimm's Cup cocktail, its amber color a perfect complement to the green expanse of lawn and trees. Although the roses, lavender delphiniums, and dignified purple foxgloves have been carefully placed and planted, the garden has an unplanned look, in the understated English way.

Henry James felt about summer afternoons the way I feel about Saturday summer mornings. I wake up on a bright, sunny day in early June here on the Mississippi Gulf Coast with a sense of anticipation. Zippity doo dah. What shall I do on this wonderful day?

"You'll go crazy," my New York and Los Angeles friends had said when I announced twelve years ago that I was moving to the South. I vehemently disagreed. "Yes, you will. You'll go mad—there's absolutely nothing to do in a sleepy southern town. It's not for you," they insisted. "Well, Jerry's for me," I countered, "so I'm going. And if it does turn out to be boring, I'll manage, because I love to read." I meant that. As much as I adore city life, I know that boredom comes from within, and as long as I have good books, fine music, and a warm friend for lively conversation, I'm happy.

But I did silently worry just a bit, "What if it's as drowsy as I've heard? What if it's worse? What if it's comatose?" Fortunately, my northeastern and West Coast friends were wrong, and I haven't suffered a moment of ennui since I've moved here.

I woke up on a recent cloudless June Saturday to the sound of hazelnut coffee beans being freshly ground. My husband was preparing our morning coffee. The aroma that always promises so much more than it delivers wafted from the kitchen to the bedroom door. I perused the local newspaper, the *Sun Herald*, and contemplated what I should do with the gift that's so easy to take for granted—another day of being alive and healthy on the Gulf Coast. On that Saturday I had plenty of possibilities, all outdoors: the Women's Soccer Championship; Gulf Coast Billfish Classic; Coast Coliseum Summer Fair; Red, White & Blueberry Festival; Annual Blessing of the Fleet; Great Biloxi Schooner Race; Fear Not Festival (marking the beginning of the Hurricane season); and the Ocean Springs Elks Junior Fishing Rodeo.

As it is for many Americans, Saturday is a busy day for me. Between grocery shopping, picking up dry cleaning, getting my hair done, catching up on e-mails and snail mail, doing laundry, and other errands, I didn't have much free time. And we had an early dinner engagement with friends. So I'd have to choose only one activity on this day. I'm not a sporty type, so I wasn't interested in the soccer or fishing events, but the blueberry festival, the summer fair, and the Blessing of the Fleet tempted me. I decided on the fourth annual Red, White & Blueberry Festival at the Ocean Springs Fresh Market, where I could get some of my food shopping done and simultaneously support the local farmers.

Against the backdrop of the one hundred-year-old white and green L&N Depot, stalls brimming with plump fresh blueberries filled the parking lot. There, on the site of the old train depot, the Fresh Market makes its home every Saturday morning. I chatted with blueberry farmers and learned that blueberries are one of the few fruits that are indigenous to our country; early Native Americans used them for medicinal purposes. I strolled by a group of people who apparently couldn't wait to get home with their berries, their lips a telltale blue-violet. In addition to blueberries, there were strawberries and free vanilla ice cream. A pyramid of green, yellow, and red bell peppers beckoned me to an umbrella-shaded stand. Since these vividly colored vegetables were in their natural, unwaxed state, I wouldn't have to scrub so hard to remove the film that coats much grocery store produce. Locals and tourists bought and sold and laughed and sipped cold drinks together. Live music made the market even more festive. Tom Beavers and Friends played blues and southern rock. When they took a break, Triage took over with acoustic folk and soft rock music.

It was a vibrant market! Here were vendors selling goat cheese and farmers selling tomatoes; there were beef jerky cooks, and beekeepers with honey; candle makers; Italian cookie bakers, and okra and squash vendors. You could buy ferns and lush foliage from plant nurseries, pralines, artisan breads, and chili peppers, Italian specialties, jams, jellies, pickles, and relishes. Diane Claughton, who is a chef and former restaurateur, was quickly selling out of her home-baked specialties, as she always does.

Every Saturday year-round, regardless of weather, you'll find Diane and Charlotte Fraisse at the Ocean Springs Fresh Market, which they founded in 2004. I'm not surprised these ladies spearheaded this venture, since Diane is an Englishwoman and Charlotte an American who lived many years in France. The bustling open air markets in European village and town squares represent a venerable tradition, with a charm that no supermarket can match. Diane and Charlotte had to close the market after Hurricane Katrina pounded the Gulf Coast in August 2005, but Margaret Miller, the executive director of the Oceans Springs Chamber of Commerce, helped these ladies reopen the following year.

JOKES ABOUT SOUTHERN CUISINE ridicule everything from the ubiquitous aspic to the essential can of mushroom soup. Cookbook author Robert St. John addresses this issue best in his delightful book, *Deep South Staples: Or How to Survive in a Southern Kitchen Without a Can of Cream of Mushroom Soup*. The first recipe he created for the book was a substitute for canned cream of mushroom soup—Mushroom Béchamel Sauce, a flavorful invention with real cream and fresh mushrooms that transforms traditional southern casseroles into gourmet delights. (It freezes well, too!) The acclaimed chef followed up that book with *Deep South Parties: Or How to Survive the Southern Cocktail Hour Without a Box of French Onion Soup Mix, a Block of Processed Cheese, or a Cocktail Weenie*. St. John grew up in Hattiesburg, where he's now a restaurateur, and he has a profound appreciation of down-home southern recipes for everything from chicken and dumplings to corn bread, banana pudding, and ham biscuits. He's a master of these southern standards as well as of elegant New South dishes.

I haven't experienced any of the 1950s convenience-food mentality here. Fortunately, I arrived after the period when dozens of dishes featured marshmallows as a staple. When I landed in south Mississippi in mid-1998, I found that the food rivaled the best of any other state I had visited. But it wasn't just the quality of the food that surprised me; I discovered that southern cuisine has a distinctly different taste because of the melding of cultures in this region.

The slow-food movement has taken hold here. Diane Claughton is such a staunch advocate that she founded Slow Foods Gulf Coast. The creed of the slow-food movement is that we must take time to savor fresh, local seasonal food at the table with family and friends. With the increase of fast-food chains in America over the last few decades, many people don't even know what a fresh, off-the-farm tomato tastes like. I didn't. Now I understand one of the reasons farmers markets are invaluable.

Agriculture has been the South's essential industry since the region was settled, and that is probably a principal reason this area has maintained its wonderful food culture. But in my decade here, I've seen even the sleepy South begin to rush its eating habits, and there's danger of losing our food heritage. When I see young professionals driving with a coffee cup in one hand, steering with the other, while talking into their speaker phones as they zip along the highway, I want to stop them with these words of Henry Ward Beecher: "No matter what looms ahead, if you can eat today, enjoy the sunlight today, mix good cheer with friends today, enjoy it and bless God for it."

The proliferation of corporate farms and the resulting demise of the American family farm is our loss. Farming is difficult and risky, but it's manifestly rewarding for those who want to maintain their independence and their connection to the soil. I was standing in line at an airport and a young man from Tennessee told me how disheartened he was that he couldn't continue his family's farming tradition because he wasn't able to compete with industrial farms. I had always heard once you get a person off the farm, they never return to it. In many cases that may be true, but that young man's passion for farming his land was intense and moving. At that moment in the Nashville International Airport, I understood his way of life was a part of the American experience we must not lose.

The smiling vendors at the farmer's market have that same love of husbandry. Shopping for victuals is a different experience when you converse with the person who raises the goats from which you get the cheese. And who would have thought I'd ever have a conversation with a beekeeper? The Gautier Gold

Honey vendor comes to the Ocean Springs Fresh Market every Saturday. After I watched an episode of *Sixty Minutes* that taught me about the importance of bees and the threats they face, I saw her work with new eyes. Honey fresh from the hive is something I couldn't have experienced or appreciated had I limited my shopping to the supermarket chains.

I flashed back to Munich, 1989. I was at the Viktualienmarkt, the massive open-air market in the city center. Standing next to me was a tall Arab woman clad in an all-black dress, known as an Abayah. It covered her from her shoulders to her feet. She was wearing a solid gold mask. She was accompanied by two women dressed identically, but wearing masks made of simple fabric. The tall lady pointed to what she wanted, never uttering a word. The other two women did the buying. The Viktualienmarkt began in 1807 as an herb market. Now hundreds of vendors sell everything from meats, cheeses, wines, produce, and flowers to an array of delicious prepared foods. A cheese vendor I met there told me his family's cheese-making tradition dates back to the beginnings of the market.

My appreciation of outdoor markets started with my first trip to Paris. When I was growing up in New York, we had one or two open-air markets, but they were small and utilitarian and hardly worth the walk. It was easier to go to the local supermarket for groceries and then pick up fresh rye bread and hard rolls at the bakery next door. But years later, in Paris, I experienced the flower market adjacent to the Seine near Notre Dame Cathedral. The profusion of delicate pink, snow white, and yellow blossoms enchanted me, and I loved strolling in the sunshine in the midst of a market that had been there since Napoleon's time.

IT WAS LUNCHTIME in Ocean Springs and I was getting a little hungry. Kenny Ward of the eponymous restaurant was grilling skinless duck breast enveloped in a delicious blueberry reduction sauce. Debbie Patout, the owner of Rene's Quality Meats and Cajun Specialties, created blossom croissants with crème brûlée and fresh, locally grown blueberries. Fortified and exhilarated, I left the market at 1:00 p.m. and went about my regular Saturday afternoon rounds. As I checked off each task on my to-do list, I was glad that I had spent the morning at the Fresh Market, but a little regretful that I had missed part of the Blessing of the Fleet festivities, which included a fais do-do, an all-day street party on the Biloxi Town Green. No one is quite certain of the fais do-do's word origin. The words stem from a French expression, that much is known. Apparently, early Cajuns held a fais do-do to proclaim their daughter's availability for marriage, often on a young woman's fifteenth birthday. It was a spirited get-together of friends and family—a festival of dancing and music—with the watchful eyes of the elders who acted as chaperones. Musicians played instruments as difficult as the violin, and as simple as the washboard, spoons, and triangle. Next year, the fais do-do!

It was a gorgeous balmy evening as I headed home. The crickets were out in full force. Another splendid Saturday on the Mississippi Gulf Coast was ending. The night lay ahead.

The Pride of
Wanda Place

WANDA PLACE is a circle of twenty-three houses built in the mid-1950s. Quiet and lined with oak
and pine trees, our street has the clean-cut feel of that
era. The only sounds in our neighborhood are cheer-
ful ones—children riding bicycles, lawnmowers hum-
ming on Saturday mornings, neighbors greeting one
another as they walk their dogs, and birds chirping.
Nice sounds—sleepy, soft sounds. So we could easily
hear his cry from across the street.

He meowed so plaintively. He was orange and
snowy white, and he was sitting in our neighbor
Mike's driveway. "He's clearly in distress," Jerry said.
Although he wore no collar, he looked as if he had
once belonged to someone. But the cat was afraid to
come near us. We put cat food and a water dish outside our door. I meowed to encourage him to come
nearer. He began to trust me and ventured closer.

Eventually, hunger got the best of him and he cautiously approached and began eating.

There's a strong sense of community on Wanda Place, even among those who don't know each other well, with people helping each other in the event of illness and watching the homes of neighbors who are out of town. The only people on the street are the ones who belong here. So a stranger is easy to spot— even when the stranger is a little cat. A few days later, Jane, a neighbor from down the street knocked on our door and introduced herself.

"We have to decide what to do with this cat," she said.

"We do?"

Jane suggested we give it to the animal shelter. Fearing that the humane society would euthanize it, however, I placed an ad in the paper, seeking its owner. I received one phone call, but the caller's missing kitty wasn't the pussycat on our street. So the cat stayed. We named him O.C., for Outside Cat. Under the guardianship of Jane, our other neighbor Pat, and my husband and me, O.C. ate well and lingered contentedly around our houses.

But I'm getting ahead of myself. The cat saga actually began a little earlier with a gray Tabby who showed up at our door with innocent, imploring eyes. Statue-still and silent, he stared at us, unblinking, through the screen door. The next day, Jerry and I bought cat food and placed it on the outside steps, and he began showing up daily. But he was easily frightened and wouldn't allow us to pet him. Jerry and I didn't want to have cats in the house, but we worried about the Tabby in case it might rain, so we bought him a doghouse. About a week later, while I was chatting with Pat in her front yard, the Tabby appeared, looking relaxed. "Do you know that cat?" I asked, as I watched him saunter toward her flowerbeds.

"Oh, that's Henry."

Aahh, so it was Pat's cat!

"Well yes, he's an outside cat," she said. He showed up at our door one day."

Pat already owned a pair of Maine Coon cats, Mike and Mitzi, and she was happy to feed another one. So Pat, Jane, Jerry and I were all feeding Henry and then O.C. As O. C. became less frightened, he befriended Henry, and that was nice because Henry seemed less scared when O.C. was around.

One day I noticed that Henry was gaining weight. Knowing that a cat doesn't usually have a beer belly, I walked over to Pat's house and passed along my observation. With her usual equanimity, Pat said, "Oh, my, then I guess we'd better call him Henrietta!" No wonder Henrietta was calm around O.C. In a few months, we saw miniature versions of O.C. running around. Each kitten was cuter than the next, but around six or eight weeks later, all except one disappeared; only the calico was left. We don't know what happened to the other sweet kittens, but Calico stayed close to her mother and displayed a very gentle disposition.

Jerry and I still didn't want to have cats in the house, but the nights were getting chilly, and all our feline visitors disdained the doghouse. So we bought a kitty condo and placed it outside our door. Calico loved sleeping in the condo, and Henrietta perched herself on top of it.

I soon learned that cats are not the only creatures that enjoy life in Mississippi neighborhoods. Though I had found and rescued several cats in New York, I had no experience with raccoons or opossums. Our driveway ends at what I've named "the Jungle" because the foliage is dense and wild. Directly behind it is Coffee Creek, a charming name, but I have never set foot near there. Our neighbor Corey tells me that snakes live there, and I believe him. This is also where raccoons dwell and, as I write this, a mother raccoon steals the cat food daily. Because she has five adorable little fur-ball babies, I let her get away with it for now. They're a nuisance, but I find the little ones endearing.

It's usually a peaceable kingdom around here. But not always. Pat placed a wooden cradle—the one she had played with as a child—on her front steps because Mitzi prefers sleeping in fresh air. One balmy evening, Mitzi padded up the stairs and found a raccoon sleeping in her bed. She smacked that little black-eyed creature, who zoomed out of there and headed for the trees. Mitzi, the matriarch, had won that battle once and for all.

Although O.C. is a good-natured tomcat, he frequently got into fights. He bore the scars of battle well. One evening, when he appeared at our house during his customary dinner hour, I saw that the swelling in his cheek I had noticed the day before had gotten worse. I lured him indoors, closed off the porch and put the kitty condo and O.C. inside. Listlessly, he crept into it and hunkered down. Jane was experienced with felines, so I called her. She jumped into action. Although she had worked since early morning and it was now late at night, she telephoned her friend, Janna, and the two of them took O.C. to the veterinarian's emergency room. The vet treated his infection and prescribed a course of antibiotics. Jane nursed him back to health; he healed; and after a suitable period of time, we had him "fixed." This has now become standard operating procedure on Wanda Place. We all tried to find a home for him. Jane's cat, Sheba, was used to being alone and wasn't about to share her royal space. In the end, Jane succumbed to O.C.'s charm, took him in, and he now prospers there, occupying a separate wing of the house from Sheba.

A short time after O.C.'s deliverance, a solemn gray and white cat appeared. He has blurry eyes and a very pink nose. He always looks as if he has a cold. Jerry named him Earl Gray. Jerry and I bought another kitty condo.

My husband has dubbed our house Beastro Read. A turtle comes occasionally to eat beside the cats and they look at him (or her—who can tell?) with a mixture of curiosity and indifference, and then nonchalantly resume eating. After breakfast the assorted kitties begin their neighborhood promenade. The squirrels then cautiously creep down from the trees to start the second breakfast shift. And the birds descend to finish all that remains.

Jerry calls the kitties "The Pride" because they behave like a group of miniature lions. The Pride used to return at noon for lunch, and then again for a mid-afternoon snack, but we stopped the twilight feedings when the raccoons became too bold. The first few days of this rationing surprised Henrietta, O.C., and Calico, who went to their little blue bowls, found nothing and looked at me, their tails formed into question marks. Perhaps they were disgruntled now because these elegant creatures were eating only five daily meals instead of six.

In the late afternoons, the cats congregate to sun themselves on our outside stairs. Calico likes to sit on the hood of my car, surveying her domain. When she sees something that makes her tense, her tail twitches in a staccato as if it had been electrified. And I can always tell when Pat's out of town, because the dignified Mitzi and her brother Mike join The Pride on our steps, yowling because they miss Pat.

When I lived in Manhattan, on the thirty-sixth floor, I was above it all. But when I moved to Mississippi, I was at street level and suddenly there were "neighborhood cats." And although I've always been an animal lover, I've never had nor wanted to be owned by a pet. Now, I found myself feeding, petting, watering, and generally caring for a congregation of cats. It's an unexpected dividend of living in Mississippi.

Not long ago, a beautiful young, shy cat appeared. She looks like an ocelot. In no time the comely lass was pregnant. With the exception of Henrietta's litter, fathered by O.C., every single cat in Wanda Place looks suspiciously like Earl Gray. We had the handsome devil neutered, and for good measure, we had Ocelot Kitty spayed. By this time, fall was rustling in, and we had not seen Mike (Mitzi's brother) for many months. I warily asked Pat if he was "still with us." "No," she said, "I'm afraid something has happened to him." We were distressed to think that Mike had died. Imagine Pat's joy—and ours, too—when, almost a year later, Mike reappeared, meowing in front of Pat's door, demanding his dinner. She asked him where he'd been for so long. He wouldn't tell her. Maybe he's part Australian and went "walkabout." He has a gorgeous deep sable coat with ermine-colored hind legs. He is one elegant and expensive-looking cat.

Cats are not the sole rulers of our enclave. On one of his morning walks, my husband met Phyllis as she walked her Scottish terrier, Laddie. Phyllis was so devoted to Laddie that she even brushed his teeth. That is unusual, but the minute you laid eyes on her dog, you understood Phyllis's affection for the aging little canine. He strolled along on his short legs, stopped to examine the flowers, and sniffed the coastal morning air. Laddie was a mellow dog whose dark eyes exuded benevolence. He was starting to go gray. Jerry called him "The General" because, he said, "Laddie looks like a general. He is stately, walks slowly, and looks as if he would be cool under pressure." We all grieved when Laddie died in January 2009.

One day Jerry stopped to admire the Christmas wreath on Phyllis's door. It was emblazoned with the silhouette of a Scottie and was attached to the door, just above the Scottie doorknocker. Phyllis invited him into her house to look at the rest of her Christmas decorations. When my husband crossed the threshold, he found himself enveloped in a world of objects honoring Phyllis's noble and beloved Laddie. Besides the Scottie Christmas ornaments, surrounding him were Scottie statues, dishtowels, paintings, napkins, potholders, books, calendars, plates, posters, mugs, needlepoint, tumblers, tote bags, clocks, andirons, firewood tools, a hooked rug, and photos of Laddie. As Jerry stood in the middle of Scottieville, Phyllis's husband walked in, and Phyllis introduced him. "This is my husband Scotty."

Phyllis and Scott now provide a happy home for Ocelot Kitty's offspring. Phyllis has named them, "fixed" them, and added them to the pride that lives in their yard and under the house and to the two who live inside. Earl Grey even allows Phyllis to pet him—something we never managed to do. Jerry says that the kitty grapevine is buzzing with gossip about our neighborhood with its soft spot for cats. Who knows how many other incredible felines will soon be joining The Pride of Wanda Place?

Scarlett O'Hara
Lives

ONE AUTUMN AFTERNOON in New York, when I was fourteen years old, I went to the movies with a girlfriend to see *Gone with the Wind*. On that occasion, we joined the international ranks of young females who, since 1939, have first glimpsed a southern belle on the big screen. In the hands of Vivian Leigh, what a glimmer it was! But film is a deceptive medium and, although I was impressionable, I knew that Margaret Mitchell's creation was fiction.

As I grew older, I questioned whether the Scarlett O'Hara and *Steel Magnolia* images were genuine prototypes of southern women or mere stereotypes. After living on the Mississippi Gulf Coast for a number of years and traveling to other parts of the South, I saw that many women in the South are indeed lovely belles who create beautiful homes, love to cook, and entertain with flair. But, I wondered, are they as unshakeable as Scarlett was? Do they possess that powerful combination of strong will and delicate femininity?

We have strong women all over our country, of course. It's a rare family where the woman is not the anchor of the household, passing the torch of stability from mother to daughter for generations. This is, I believe, the reason husbands tend to be absorbed into wives' families. I was familiar with the literature of pioneer women who left East Coast cities to follow their husbands west. An old William Wellman film entitled *Westward the Women* tells the story of one hundred thirty-eight Chicago women who crossed America in wagon trains to the California Valley. They undertook the arduous journey to seek husbands. I knew about Yankee women who demonstrated tremendous capability and courage in the settling of our nation. One of the best American novels ever written, *My Antonia*, by Willa Cather, describes the struggles of a group of immigrant families when they move to rural Nebraska. Although this book is a fictionalized account of homesteading the prairies, it gives an accurate picture of what women had to contend with during Western expansionism. Disease-bearing insects in the summer, blizzards in the winter, loneliness, and the challenges of farming were just a few of the hardships the women faced. They met their plights bravely as they created new lives.

But I didn't know any real southern women who faced such adversity and succeeded with their femininity intact. The South's male historical figures are famous, but I knew so little of its women. I began to get curious about southern women. I read and talked to southerners and became intrigued by what I learned. How is it that I had never heard of Elizabeth Lee Hazen? Born in Rich, Mississippi, in 1885, Hazen lived a long and productive life as an important microbiologist, dying in 1975 at the age of ninety. She weathered enormous struggles. Orphaned at the age of three, she lived in a poverty-stricken town where she attended a one-room school. But her intelligence and determination prevailed. In association with the New York scientist, Rachel Fuller Brown, Hazen invented Nystatin, an antifungal/antibiotic still in use today.

I found that other accomplished southern women had overcome serious hardships to succeed. Katherine Anne Porter, who wrote *Ship of Fools*, *Pale Horse, Pale Rider*, and other books and short stories, also lived to be ninety (1890–1980), and she lost her mother when she was two years old. She and her four siblings lived with her paternal grandmother until she died when Porter was eleven. Her father was unable or unwilling to pay attention to his children, and she was shuttled to a variety of Texas and Louisiana convent schools—a difficult beginning for a child. In addition to her acclaim as a writer, Katherine Anne Porter was well-known for her feminine qualities.

Carson McCullers, the author of *The Heart is a Lonely Hunter, The Ballad of the Sad Café, The Member of the Wedding,* and *Reflections in a Golden Eye,* lived only fifty years (1917–1967). Born in Columbus, Georgia, she gained fame as a woman of letters in spite of a lifetime of poor health. At fifteen, she contracted rheumatic fever; at twenty-four, she endured the first of a number of strokes that impaired her vision and left her slightly paralyzed. And at the age of thirty, she suffered a sequence of strokes that made it impossible for her to type with both hands. By the age of thirty-one, she was totally paralyzed on her left side.

The remarkable Josephine Baker (1906–1975) and her washerwoman mother were abandoned by Josephine's father shortly after her birth. Although her mother later married a good-natured man, he was constantly unemployed, and Josephine began working at the age of eight, cleaning houses and babysitting. She dropped out of school when she was twelve, and at thirteen, obtained a job as a waitress, living for a year as a street child in the St. Louis slums and finding food wherever she could, including garbage cans. She danced on street corners, finally gaining attention at the age of fifteen, when the St. Louis Chorus vaudeville show engaged her for their chorus line. Intrepid, she soon moved to New York, where the

Harlem Renaissance was in full swing, and garnered praise for her nightclub performances. Four years later, she moved to Paris, and became the center of the European entertainment world as a glamorous dancer and singer.

The successful southern women mentioned above, who suffered adversity and met it with Scarlett O'Hara determination, are but a few of many I've read about or known. The stories of extremely successful women who come largely from rural southern states, however, were new to me. Whether from Arkansas or Mississippi, Louisiana or Tennessee, the admirable women I've met have had to fight harder than their northern peers for career success. They've had to be more tenacious to achieve economic independence. The South suffered more than its share of poverty. And southern women who are in their fifties or sixties today had a greater struggle for recognition outside of the domestic realm because the mindset of people south of the Mason-Dixon line was generally conservative.

I was astonished to learn, for example, that a Mississippi woman graduating from college in the middle to late 1960s often had only two socially acceptable career choices: teaching or nursing. A Mississippi friend told me that at her thirty-fifth college reunion, all of the women in that class, except one, ended up as teachers. I've met southern women of that generation and older who ventured into traditionally male professions, but most moved up North to pursue them. A woman from the Northeast who was in college in the 1960s had the opportunity to be anything she wanted to be, from an architect to a zoologist. She had the "glass ceiling" to work through, but she began with the assumption that a woman could pursue and achieve excellence in any career that interested her.

I'm pleased to know that southern women have come into their own since the 1960s. In the following chapter I write about one such woman, Nancy, who entered college in 1970, and after decades of hard work, she's a successful and fulfilled wife, mother, and professional woman. I consider her the archetypal modern southern woman. Is it any surprise that she, too, had a strong southern mother?

Let us now praise southern women.

A Class Act

"THERE ARE NO SECOND ACTS in American life," F. Scott Fitzgerald said. But he didn't know Nancy Larrison Campbell.

Nancy has all-American Irish good looks, and she is happily married to a successful lawyer. Nancy and Roy Campbell have three lovely grown daughters. The Campbell's stately columned home in Jackson, Mississippi, is worthy of an *Architectural Digest* spread, and Nancy enjoys her career as a doctor. Nothing in her appearance or lifestyle hints at a rebellious nature. But Nancy always did everything a little bit differently, such as entering medical school when she was forty-four years old.

Wilmot, Arkansas, had a population of 721 when Nancy Larrison was born to Aline and Clifford Larrison in 1952. Today its residents number 706. Wilmot had no restaurant. The nearest hospital was thirty miles away, in Lake Village, Arkansas, but it had no OB-GYN department, so Nancy was born sixty miles away, across the Mississippi River, in Greenville, Mississippi. Her father had two siblings, both straight-A students. Clifford considered himself the black sheep of the family. By 1957 he had held one job after another and struggled to make ends meet. Then one day, he was asked to manage a farm in Cuba. Clifford seized the opportunity.

So off they went—Clifford, Aline, almost five-year-old Nancy, and her twelve-year-old brother—with Della, Nancy's babysitter, in tow. Della's presence on the trip was a surprise to the family. "On the morning we were leaving she showed up with a suitcase and announced that she was going with us because she knew that we needed her," Nancy said. "We couldn't afford her, but she said she would go for free. She climbed into the car, and that was that."

To this Arkansas Delta child, Camaguey, Cuba, was a revelation. One of the first municipalities established by the Spaniards in the sixteenth century, it had a population of approximately 625,000 when Nancy's family moved there in 1957. Unlike her tiny southern hometown, Camaguey offered to this bright and energetic little girl an opportunity for constant activity. Batista's Cuba opened a fascinating, idyllic new world. Nancy loved her new home but hated kindergarten because she couldn't understand

Spanish. "So the first day I climbed over the fence during recess and started walking home," she said. "My parents called the police, and a police car carrying Della found me. I was taken back a second day and escaped again. After that, my parents decided that I would just skip kindergarten."

Their house was on a city street, very close to the road, with neighbors close by coming and going. She recalled the vibrant life on the street and the local Cuban people she could talk to.

"You could run out with some money to buy a banana or some ice cream. I used to sit in the window of our living room, between the glass and the iron bars, watch the street traffic, and talk to the postman when he delivered the mail. During naptime, I'd stand on my bed and talk through the open window with the gardener, who taught me how to count in Spanish."

"CASTRO HAS LANDED."

With those words, Della awakened Nancy's parents in the middle of the night. It was December 31, 1958. Della had just returned from a neighbor's house two doors down, where she had forged a friendship with the houseboy, whose employer was a friend of Fidel Castro. He informed Della that Castro had come down from the hills with his brother Raúl, Che Guevara, and a band of rebels; they were using guerilla warfare tactics and attacking Batista's forces, and overtaking villages and towns. The Larrisons roused Nancy and her brother Jim and said, "Here are your suitcases. We have to pack your clothes." Knowing that Castro would take everything, they fled. Early the next morning, they took a boat back to the United States. A week later Castro and his army took control of Havana. Her father had left behind the farm equipment he had purchased for the Cuban farm. When he returned to retrieve it, he was turned away empty-handed. Not for the first time in his life, Clifford Larrison lost everything.

After being in Cuba only a little more than a year, the Larrisons were back in Wilmot, Arkansas. Nancy's parents, penniless, read the Bastrop (LA) *Daily Enterprise* looking for jobs. Nancy entered the first grade in Wilmot and repeated her Cuban antics. She left during recess and went downtown. After that, her parents dispatched Della to accompany Nancy and stay with her all day to ensure that she didn't leave. Eventually, they sent Nancy's German shepherd Dixie with her. Dixie sat in the classroom next to Nancy's desk. This enforcement method continued until Nancy finished the third grade. Dixie's attendance even earned her a picture in the school yearbook.

LIKE ALMOST ALL of the southern women I've known, Nancy is an excellent cook. After an especially deli-

cious meal at Roy and Nancy's one night, I complimented her culinary skill. Curled up in her den with
an after-dinner drink in hand, she dismissed her talents in the kitchen. "I remember everybody in
Wilmot was a good cook, and they were effortless
cooks." Since the tiny town had no restaurants, all
the cooking had to be done at home. "It never
occurred to me that I wouldn't cook," she continued,
"although I was never in the kitchen growing up
because we always had a cook." And this is another
interesting side of the southern experience. Even
though her family had little money in her early years,
they always had a cook working in the kitchen.

The close relationship between black domestics
and their white employers is one of the most complex
aspects of southern culture. Northerners don't understand it, and it's nearly impossible to explain. To an
outsider, it seems that a segregated society would pre-
clude affection across the racial divide between
employer and employee. But the reality was far more
complicated. "Everybody knew everyone else's cook.
They were certainly part of the family," Nancy
explained. During one especially difficult year, the
Larrisons couldn't afford to keep Della, so Nancy's
grandmother took care of her. It didn't work out well.
When Della saw how unhappy the family was, she
returned the following year to work without pay. She
continued to live in her own house but, as was the

custom, Della ate all meals at the Larrisons' house during the work day. Later on, when her family was in better financial condition, they paid Della for all the time she had worked for them without pay.

Our country has changed much over the last forty years, and the South has probably changed the most. Nancy remembers segregation and the strange situations she found herself in. "One time Della was taking me to the doctor, and when we got to the waiting room doors, she said, 'Well, you'll go in here, and I'll go in there,' motioning to the "colored entrance." I said, 'But I want you to go with me,' and she told me, 'I can't go in the door you go in.' So I said, 'Well, I'll go in your door.' I was allowed to go in the door marked 'Colored,' but Della couldn't go in the 'Whites Only' door. So I would wait in the black waiting room with Della until they called my name. In later years, when my parents had more money, we would go out of town to eat, and Della would go to the kitchen of the restaurant; I would go sit with Della in the kitchen, which was much more fun than sitting out front with my parents."

After they returned on the boat from Cuba, Aline was driving Nancy, her brother, and Della home from Miami. (Her father had taken the boat with them to Miami but had returned immediately to try to salvage his farm equipment.) "Mother stopped at hotel after hotel to spend the night," Nancy recalled. "She'd go in and say, 'I'd like a room or two, and I've got my children's nurse with me.' But they wouldn't let Della spend the night, and mother would get in the car and go to the next one. And again she said, 'Okay, we'll go to the next one.' Afterwards, Mother told me, 'I just couldn't have Della stay out in the car by herself.' So we drove all night."

Nancy vividly remembers the day she went to Della's house and saw the awful living standard of her caretaker. I suspect this was a pivotal moment for Nancy, awakening her social conscience. "Her first home in Wilmot was about a block from ours; it was pretty much a wooden shack, with bare floors and probably very little insulation," Nancy said. Fortunately, several years later Della acquired another house through a federal grant. Also located in town, it was a new, small brick home with living room, kitchen, three bedrooms, and a bath. "Della was a master cleaner," Nancy said. "She really, honestly loved to clean and was the best cleaner I've ever seen. Both homes were spotlessly maintained with polished floors and not a speck of dust or one thing out of place."

When Nancy was in the sixth grade, her mother and Della had a "big falling out" and Mrs. Larrison fired Della. "I must have sobbed for two or three weeks because it was like my mother being taken away from me. My mother had always worked, and it just broke my heart," Nancy recalled. She never learned what the disagreement was about. "Immediately after Della was fired, she went to California to see her sister, Tea, and stayed there. And I visited her there while I was staying with my cousin, who lived in Arcadia, California," Nancy remembered. About five years later, however, Della returned to Wilmot and worked for Nancy's brother Jim and his wife Sherlyn.

"Della grew up on a farm outside Wilmot," Nancy said. "Her mother died when she was young, and Della said that after her mother died, her mother appeared to her one day outside the house and told Della that she was doing fine." As I listened to Nancy, I pictured Della—with her small nose and big smile that revealed one gold tooth—laughing and joking with Nancy, all those years ago. And when I imagine a vulnerable little Nancy crying her eyes out, I understand how wrenching this sudden dismissal of Della must have been.

My husband appreciates the tremendous affection between Nancy and Della. His own family had a deep love for Hallie, who, like Della, cleaned the house, cooked, and babysat. When Hallie became old and ill, Jerry's mother took care of her. These children's caretaker was, Jerry says, a "co-Mom."

Meanwhile, Aline Larrison had had enough struggle. When Nancy was in the third grade, her mother learned that a nearby farm was for sale, and she insisted that Clifford buy it. Always willing to try a new venture, her father made an offer that the farmer accepted. So Clifford went to his father, the bank president, to borrow money for the purchase. The senior Larrison refused his son's request, reminding Clifford that he had always been a failure. When Gus Pugh, the owner of the bank, heard about Clifford's dilemma, he offered him a personal loan. Clifford Larrison's charisma, which would serve him well throughout his life, had worked its magic. He would not let Mr. Pugh down.

Before embarking on this project, her dad would have to find help. "When Daddy first started, he had not one penny. He couldn't afford a worker, so he went to Cummins Prison (where Johnny Cash later performed) and got a black parolee named Louis. All he had to do to get Louis was say he'd give him a job. So he and Louis cleared Daddy's first farm, which was a swamp. Everybody said it wouldn't be able to grow rice. But for some reason Daddy thought it would," Nancy said. "And it did actually. So he and Louis cleared two thousand acres of land with a bulldozer. And my father was five foot seven and weighed 140 pounds."

IT WAS UNCOMMON for southern women to work outside of the home when Nancy was growing up in the 1950s and 60s, but Nancy's mother, Aline, had always worked as a bookkeeper. According to Nancy, "Mother grew up very poor and worked her way through college and got everywhere she got by the hard scrabble of herself. And she was really smart and very capable. I think that's why my father was eventually a financial success. I think Mother just felt she had to get right in there and do the details." Her father always attributed his success to her mother and Gus Pugh. "Daddy's charming and he's got great ideas. There's a lot that's really admirable about Daddy. He'd get knocked down and get right back up and be knocked down again. But he always got back up. And finally he and mother together made a success of the farm."

"And then suddenly we were well-off," Nancy said.

The rapid social ascent that accompanied their prosperity confused Nancy; after all, she was the same person she had always been. "We were very poor until I was in about the third or fourth grade. And then farming took off, and by the time I was in about the sixth grade we were doing very well, so I got to see the whole gamut. I got to see the hand-me-down clothes that came from someplace and that I pulled out and my mother said, 'Oh, this is so awful.' But I had to wear them anyway. And then all of a sudden I was going to the rich girl's camp in Wisconsin with the daughter of a General Motors executive." This drastic transformation taught her to distrust people's perceptions about social status.

The Larrisons reveled in their newfound wealth. First, they gave Della her back pay. And her parents loved dining out. The nearest restaurant was sixty miles away, and Nancy's parents always took her with them. "It would be my parents and another couple—always two couples and me. We all piled into the car—the first nice car we had was a blue Bonneville convertible—and no one worried about drinking and driving back then, so they'd drink all the way over to the restaurant. They'd tell stories and laugh, and then we'd eat, and on the way back they'd rehash the night. I just listened. And after a while, they would forget that I was there. I learned all sorts of things. I can remember going to New Orleans with my parents and Frances Shackelford (who was from Montrose, Arkansas, and also Wilmot's society leader) and her date at the time, Thane Muller. Or the five of us would go out to the nightclubs in Hot Springs. We'd go to the 11:30 show, of course."

Although the Larrisons didn't take family vacations, her father did a lot of business in New Orleans, where he bought rice allotments. Impulsively, Clifford would wake up the family and say, "Nancy, get your clothes on, we're going to New Orleans." Or perhaps it would be San Antonio. After his farm began to flourish, Mr. Larrison acquired a tiny

Cessna airplane. So they hopped into it and took off at his behest.

FARM LIFE IN THE ARKANSAS DELTA was busy in the spring and fall. Her father grew rice and soybeans. In the spring he had to get the crop in the ground, and in the fall he had to get it out of the ground. Since there was a limited time each season to get those things done, he worked hard, long hours during those months. One hard rain at the wrong time could devastate the entire year's crop. Nancy thinks that farming attracts people like her father—those devil-may-care personalities who can live with the constant risks of farming. In the summer when the crop was growing and in the winter months, however, there was ample time for fun. To escape the monotony of the slow times, people got together and had fun. A good sense of humor and storytelling ability became valuable social skills. But who wouldn't become a little dreamy, living in the South? The climate and lush landscape invite dreams. After all, the first hammock that was manufactured in the United States was made in South Carolina.

When I woke up in Manhattan, I took my coffee out to the terrace and looked at the city from the thirty-sixth floor. The boats on the Hudson River carrying cargo, the honking cabdrivers on West Street impatiently transporting passengers to their Wall

Street offices, the pedestrians scooting between the cars, ignoring the WALK and DON'T WALK signals—those sights and sounds impelled me to jump into the shower and get going. I didn't want to be left behind! But when I moved to Ocean Springs, the first sound to greet me each morning was the bird's chirping, and the first sight was the soft blue bayou. It was a gentle beginning and I began to savor time.

In southeast Arkansas the emphasis was on social life. "And the social life there was dominated by Frances Shackelford, who was like the free-spirited aunt in the movie, *Auntie Mame*," Nancy said. "All of us knew how to mix drinks at a very early age. Frances has the best taste I've ever seen of anybody in my entire life. Her houses are unbelievable, they're interesting, and they're beautiful." Nancy added, "The Mississippi and Arkansas Delta people knew how to put on a party."

But social elegance wasn't enough to keep Nancy in Wilmot. She yearned for something more. Nancy loved books and as she read about the larger world, she discovered places that might be more suited to her nature than Arkansas. That "something more" was St. Catherine's Boarding School in Richmond, Virginia, which emphasized the importance of higher education. It had been founded in 1890 and drew many of its students from the first families of Virginia. "When I went to Richmond, it was like heaven opened up. Richmond is gorgeous. It has the prettiest architecture anywhere. And so I just thought that was heaven," Nancy said.

It was during this time that she met Roy Campbell. At a dance at Episcopal High School in Alexandria, Virginia, Nancy met Peyton Prospere, who invited her to a dance in his hometown of Greenville, Mississippi. She was delighted, and not long after that occasion, Peyton introduced her to his good friend, Roy Campbell, also from Greenville. Peyton turned out to be an excellent matchmaker.

When it was time to begin college in 1970, Nancy, at her mother's urging, chose Vanderbilt University in Nashville. Her father had always supported her dreams and encouraged her to be ambitious. In first grade, when Nancy announced that she wanted to be a nurse like her aunt, her father responded, "Don't be a nurse. Be a doctor! Lord, you can be a doctor." But the Women's Liberation Movement sweeping the country in the late 1960s was slower to take hold in the Deep South, and Nancy, like most young southern women graduating from college in that era, chose to forego a career of her own for marriage and family. After graduating magna cum laude with a degree in business, she married Roy Campbell when she was twenty-two, and they moved to Greenville, Mississippi, where he would practice law in his family's firm. She could not have known then that more than twenty years later, she would return to Vanderbilt as a medical student.

IN GREENVILLE, she applied for a job at the bank, and the bank officer who interviewed her, said. "I'm not going to hire you. You'll just join the garden club."

"You don't understand, I'm not much of a garden club type," she responded.

"Look, you'll join the garden club. You're married to Roy Campbell; you'll join the garden club."

"They just didn't think I was a good long-term investment because I was going to have babies and join the garden club." So, she devoted herself to being a wife and mother. She loved raising her children and put enormous care and energy into that role. And, she joined the garden club. But first she would join the National Council of Negro Women.

The National Council of Negro Women, the NCNW, sponsored a program called Operation Sisters United. This program was for the benefit of children who had gotten into trouble or had minor scrapes with the law, like shoplifting. Nancy was the program coordinator. The children would come to her program in the afternoon after school, and she would work with them to help them refocus their lives. When Nancy attended the national convention of the NCNW, she was the only white woman there. "And it really was a wonderful experience," she said. "I was surrounded by these vibrant, glowing, exuberant women."

Tales of bankers and garden clubs aside, Greenville, Mississippi, was in many ways an ideal place for Nancy Campbell to come into her own as a woman of intelligence and independent thinking. The Mississippi River town had always possessed a stimulating group of writers, artists, intellectuals, and eccentrics. The first mayor of Greenville was Jewish. A spirit of tolerance distinguished Greenville, a tenor established early by the Percy family and galvanized in the first half of the twentieth century by Will Percy, cousin of the writer Walker Percy. When Walker Percy's father died prematurely, his three sons—Walker, Phin, and Roy—went to live with their father's cousin, but called him "Uncle Will". Will Percy was a bachelor poet with a love of art and literature and ideas, and he entertained a host of well-traveled, well-read people from all over the world. His influence, not only upon his nephew Walker, but also upon the entire town is indisputable.

Hodding Carter, Jr., who moved to Greenville in the 1930s with his wife Betty to run the Delta *Democrat Times* newspaper, sustained the town's liberal, free-spirited atmosphere. "The Carters were known for having big parties all the time," Nancy recalled. "And they included everybody—Republicans, Democrats, people from out of town—everybody was invited. Someone told me that they didn't care what your politics were as long as you were pleasant about it." Nancy believes that the abundant creativity that defines Greenville is the result of its open-minded attitude: people can risk doing something different without fear of failure.

Nancy continued, "I remember Roy's mother used to laugh about—I've forgotten this lady's name—who went on a trip to the Mediterranean and brought a gigolo home with her, and she built a Mediterranean villa for the two of them. The Greenville people all just laughed. It wasn't as if she was excluded from the garden club. They just laughed. They were discerning; they probably thought the gigolo wasn't a great idea, but they didn't get all bent out of shape about it." A friend once told me that, in the Mississippi Delta, eccentricity is a virtue. This must be what she meant!

Even in Greenville, however, Nancy resisted authority when it didn't make sense to her. She joined the Presbyterian Church and questioned anything illogical in its teachings. So after yet another Sunday session in which she quizzed the minister, she was gently asked to leave, but not by the church. The president of the bank approached her and said, "Nancy, is there any way I can get you to stop coming to Sunday school? All my wife talks about all afternoon long is how upset you've made her, and I'm so tired of talking about you. Really, is there anything I can do so that I don't have to talk about you every Sunday afternoon?" Nancy, unmoved, continued to attend. But a few years later, "I matured a little and decided to give everyone a rest," and she stopped going. Her spiritual path has remained a solo journey.

AS NANCY AND ROY'S CHILDREN were entering their teenage years, Nancy's early ambition for a professional career resurfaced. By 1997 all the pieces were finally in place. The following year, their daughter, Larrison, would be eighteen years old, a rising senior at the Groton School in Massachusetts, and their twin daughters, Martha and Liz, who would enter the eighth grade, would soon be attending Groton. Roy had a thriving legal practice and supported Nancy's goal. Nancy applied to Vanderbilt Medical School, and she was accepted in 1997.

On her first day in medical school, each of the new students stood and introduced themselves to the others in the class. Nancy recalls, "One guy had a PhD in organic chemistry. He was a professor at Berkeley. Another one, also with a PhD, was a physics professor at Cornell; someone else had just graduated first in his class at Washington and Lee." One after another the students rose to declare their distinguished credentials and experiences. Then Nancy stood and said, "I'm a housewife in Mississippi. I was driving carpool last week."

Women in Greenville were immensely supportive of Nancy's decision. "One of the really shocking things was that my biggest supporters were the women who were about ten years older than I was. They were precisely the group I thought might have resented it. People I didn't really know that well would come up to me and say, 'I heard you're going to medical school. I think it's just great.' And now a lot of those women are my patients."

Roy moved to Nashville in 1998 and stayed until the autumn of 2001. Nancy graduated from the Vanderbilt Medical School in the summer of 2001 and immediately began the first year of her three-year residency there. When Roy moved to Jackson in the fall of 2001 to practice law, Nancy decided to complete the last two years of her three-year residency program at the University of Mississippi Medical School in Jackson, moving there in July 2002. She served the second year of her residency in Jackson, and then returned to Vanderbilt to complete her training. In June 2004, she joined a practice in Jackson.

IN THE MEANWHILE, their daughters finished high school and college and came home for holidays and vacations. Now they're all engaged in stimulating careers of their own—Larrison in the entertainment industry in Hollywood, the twins in New York, working in the art and the financial worlds. Roy's financial and emotional support was essential to making this transition possible for the entire family.

Upon finishing her residency at the age of fifty-one, Nancy joined an established medical clinic in Jackson as a specialist in internal medicine. While some of her friends are retiring or preparing to do so, Nancy Larrison Campbell, M.D. is happily fulfilling her lifelong ambition.

So, yes, Mr. Fitzgerald, there are second acts in American life.

Little White Lies

NEW YORKERS ARE DIRECT. They deal with people in an honest, gruff-friendly manner. With multitudes of human beings squeezed shoulder-to-shoulder in subway cars, crunched front-to-back in elevators, and jostling for space on the sidewalks, big city dwellers are forced to be superficially intimate. Their daily interaction with masses of people discourages formality. New Yorkers are a huge family of strangers. And this, paradoxically, makes New Yorkers friendly, albeit in a way that can be disconcerting to other Americans, especially southerners.

This peculiar friendliness manifests in various ways. New Yorkers freely ask questions or make comments to strangers whom they'll probably never see again. This is in contrast to southerners, who, though genuinely congenial, maintain a slight reserve until one has established a relationship. Here's a typical example of New York friendliness: I was walking on Eighth Avenue on a sweltering summer afternoon in Manhattan. Because New York summers are hot and humid, we usually dress accordingly. Despite the heat on that day, I was clothed in black from top to bottom—blouse, skirt, pantyhose, heels. I was headed uptown.

A truck driver inching along on the congested avenue, called out to me, "Hey, honey, aren't you hot in that?" I shook my head.

I walked another block or so and a man came from the opposite direction, and asked as he hurried by, "Lady, aren't you hot in all that black?"

I smiled.

A few blocks later, yet another man proclaimed, "You must be hot as hell in that outfit!"

These questions didn't strike me as odd. It was hot, and they were curious. But I can't imagine such an exchange occurring in Mississippi. People here might wonder why I had made that sartorial choice, but they would never have questioned me. Because the South is made up of many small communities, you'll probably run into the same people repeatedly. It would be rude to pass someone on the street and fail to greet him, even if that person is a non-acquaintance. But question my dress? I doubt it.

Julian Brunt often prepares and serves an exquisite Saturday lunch at his home in Biloxi. He regularly gathers a small group of friends, often members of the artistic-literary community—a casual southern version of the French literary salons. His guests rarely exceed six in number, so that we may all have quiet conversation. "I had a formal southern background," he said, pouring the Grüner Veltliner, an unusually good Riesling he had paired with the first course, a smoked salmon with diced red onions, capers, and crème fraîche. "I was taught to say, 'Yes Ma'am, No Sir' and to always open a door for a lady and to show respect for elders."

When Julian was thirteen years old, his parents took him on their first trip to Washington, D.C. "Mother would never have taken us on a trip like that without dressing up, so we were decked out," Julian said. His blonde cowlick "was plastered down a bit." He eagerly greeted each rushing passerby. "Hello." "Hello." "Hello." "Hello." I picture his head bobbing from one face to another, so as not to miss anyone. The pedestrians either completely ignored his salutations, or gave him hostile glances. He was astonished and bewildered. "I was stymied, but then I realized that these people were different from us. I decided that being from the South meant something after all."

All well-mannered Americans share common courtesies, but good manners arouse deeper feelings in southerners. Friends of ours, Raymond and Joy

Hunter, invited us to a pre-symphony dinner with our friend Donna. When the waiter arrived with the check, Donna tried to pay her share. "Oh, no! You're my guest!" Raymond said, just as a polite man from any other part of the country might have done. But Raymond is steeped in the traditions of a family that has lived in Mississippi for generations, and the check-paying incident had disturbed him on a level that only a chivalrous son of the South could appreciate. "Ah was horrified!" he whispered to Jerry and me afterwards.

Many outside the South assume that much southern courtesy is superficial, a cover for underlying hostilities. I can only speak from personal experience and observation, but I find polite behavior in the South stems from a heartfelt desire to please people, to have others comfortable, and, above all, to avoid hurting anyone's feelings. One case in point: Neil Spisak, a talented Hollywood production designer and friend of Lucy Denton and family, came to visit them in south Mississippi. The Dentons had a Golden Retriever, which they named Spisak after Neil, much to the delight of their California friend. Although Spisak was a sweet dog, the family couldn't train him. He was always jumping on people and creating disruption in the household. Finally, the exhausted Denton clan stopped trying to make a mannerly canine out of Spisak and gave him to a friend in

Brooklyn, Mississippi, "so he could run to his heart's content," Lucy said. They adopted another Retriever whom Will Denton named Gumps. Gumps was calm, and he had perfect manners.

Anticipating Neil Spisak's next visit from California, the Dentons were afraid that Neil's feelings would be hurt because they had deported his namesake. After all, no less an authority on manners than Emily Post, herself a southerner (from Maryland), has written, "Manners are a sensitive awareness of the feelings of others. If you have that awareness, you have good manners, no matter what fork you use." So the family did the only mannerly thing they could do—they decided that as long as Neil was in town they would refer to Gumps as Spisak. When Neil arrived, he was amazed at how well behaved the spurious Spisak had become. But poor Gumps, who was a smart dog and knew his own name, was perplexed when someone looked at him and said, "Come here, Spisak!" After a day or two, even the polite Dentons couldn't continue the charade, and they told Neil the truth. But I think even Ms. Post would have understood.

Southern hospitality is not merely about setting a beautiful table. The esthetics of welcoming a guest are important, but a southerner's desire to give her visitor joy—and above all not to offend—lies at the heart of the region's famous graciousness.

The wish to give their guests pleasure spurred the Dentons on to another duplicitous act. It was the first time that Neil, along with Gina and Jonathan (a lively New York couple), were coming to Biloxi for Mardi Gras; so Lucy bought a king cake. No Mardi Gras is complete without the sugary specialty with a tiny plastic baby baked inside. When their daughter Dawn Denton returned from a date that evening, she cut a piece of cake for herself and discovered the plastic baby in her slice. Lucy said, "Oh, put it back in the cake so we can explain the custom to our company, and one of them will get the baby."

The next day the Dentons explained the king cake tradition—that whoever finds the baby in the king cake is required to buy the next cake—and she cut a slice for each guest. Neil was tickled to find the plastic baby in his slice and for much of the day spoke of little else. After a long lunch with a great deal of wine, Neil bragged, "I got the baby, I got the baby" yet again. An exasperated Dawn admitted, "Well, Neil, you really didn't find the baby. I did, and Mom made me put it back so one of you could find it," at which point Neil threw the baby at Dawn and said, "Oh great! You buy the next cake."

And no story is too outlandish when necessity arises. When the Dentons' twin boys were young, the family had two Cocker Spaniels. One day, after dropping her boys off at school, Lucy returned home to find that one of the dogs had been run over by a car. Distraught, she called Claire, her longtime friend. "What am I to tell the boys? They'll be devastated!" Claire replied, "Just tell them the truth. Tell them that a little crippled orphan boy came by and fell in love with the dog. The orphan child had no dog, and since Jack and Walt have two dogs, you knew they would want the poor little crippled boy to have one of theirs."

The boys slept well that night, or so the story goes. . . .

Mardi Gras

"**T**HROW ME SOMETHIN'! Please, baby! Over here!" The unshaven man calling to me was on the young side of middle age. His eyes told me that he had had a hardscrabble life. I was riding on top of a Mardi Gras float that was making its way slowly through a crowd of people jamming the Gulfport streets, their arms upraised. I made eye contact, aimed, and pitched my riches to him. He caught the plastic doubloons.

What a thrill! For the first and only time, I, like the earliest Roman kings, offered "panem et circenses" to an eager crowd. "Panem et circenses," Latin for "bread and circuses," refers to the ancient annual custom in which the Roman Emperor, amid great spectacle, tossed bread and coins to the destitute masses, hoping to avoid civil unrest. Mardi Gras parades have their roots in those pre-Christian times, although the traditions in today's carnival celebrations have French-Catholic overtones related to the Nativity. But the history of Mardi Gras in New Orleans, the Mississippi Gulf Coast, and Mobile, Alabama, is as hazy as a reveler's memory the morning after a Mardi Gras ball.

Before I moved to Mississippi, I had thought of Mardi Gras strictly as a New Orleans tradition. I had no idea that there's a question whether the oldest Mardi Gras celebration in this country is in New Orleans or Mobile. The confusion lies in the ever-changing borders of the Gulf Coast. By 1704, Mobile was the capital of the French province of Louisiana. Mobile claims to have staged the first Mardi Gras parade in 1703, and this is probably true. But I caution you: don't introduce this topic in New Orleans, particularly when its citizens have been quaffing strong spirits. New Orleanians take their good times seriously, holding to their belief that they're the originators of and the rightful heirs to the greatest party in the world. The air virtually shimmers in shades of purple, green, and gold during carnival time. Drive or walk anywhere in New Orleans, south Mississippi, or coastal Alabama from January 6th (Twelfth Night, the celebration of the Epiphany) to Fat Tuesday (the day before Ash Wednesday), and you'll see reflections of these colors everywhere—on car windshields, bouncing off of store windows, and in the sequins of even the simplest costumes.

Most northerners view Mardi Gras, especially the one in New Orleans, as a drunken orgy. I had always avoided it, fearing inebriated crowds. New Orleans is a charming city, and I didn't want to spoil its romance by attending a vulgar event. But in 2003, having lived in the South for five years, I relinquished my prejudice and gratefully accepted an invitation to spend a Mardi Gras weekend with our friends Anne Jordan and Judge Tom Senter in the historic Warehouse District of New Orleans.

The first event was a nighttime parade, and we had a choice spot for catching the mementos that people threw from the floats. Behind me, the sound of Fats Domino's "Walking to New Orleans" floated out of an apartment window. Against the backdrop of a night sky, the costumes glittered. But this was a small parade, our friends said, merely an inkling of what we would see the following day, when all the major krewes (private nonprofit clubs) would be out in full regalia.

MARDI GRAS DAY BEGAN inauspiciously. The sky was gray, and a drizzly rain fell. I was uncomfortable walking in the damp, chilly air. And my naturally arrow-straight hair was beginning to frizz. That was really annoying! But I quietly ambled along as we strolled among the thickening crowd. I began to hear percussive music. We turned a corner, and I was dumbstruck.

The heart of the French Quarter looked like the set of a Fellini film. Court jesters in brilliant yellow were carousing alongside kings with burgundy capes; a princess swathed in lavender chiffon flirted with a pirate; a queen in a black ball gown etched in silver was talking with a mysterious figure wearing a gold mask. Music blared and people danced. The costumes in the densely-packed street were just as lavish as those on the floats. Even the friendly mules pulling carriages wore fancy harnesses and little straw hats. I saw one or two risqué outfits on Bourbon Street, but no one behaved badly. The streets oozed contagious good fellowship.

Now, I've seen some fabulous costumes in my time. Living in Los Angeles was often like watching an amusement show. But the imaginative Halloween outfits in West Hollywood were simple compared to these extravagant confections. Mardi Gras sets the ultimate stage for the best costume designers, jewelry makers, wig makers and make-up artists, allowing them to fully display their talents. A dazzling woman walked by in a sumptuous midnight-blue velvet eighteenth-century French gown, billowing over at least a dozen petticoats. The bodice dipped at the waist, where it was etched in crystals; the sleeves were gathered at the elbows and trimmed with the same crystals. She wore matching earrings, necklace, and bracelet. Her Marie Antoinette wig towered above her head, probably a full three feet. The wig, white with a silvery-blue undertone, was adorned with midnight blue plumes. I thought of a deep blue starry sky.

I HAD CAUGHT MY FIRST close-up glimpse of carnival artistry when the Walter Anderson Museum of Art in Ocean Springs mounted a Mardi Gras exhibit. There are many gifted costume designers on the Gulf Coast, but few of them approach Carter Church's fame and artistry. Museum director Marilyn Lyons arranged to showcase his work. As the museum's public affairs director, I expected to enjoy planning media coverage for this project. But I was completely unprepared for what I saw. I literally caught my breath when Carter carefully pulled out a Mardi Gras queen's shimmering gown, which he and his two seamstresses had hand-embellished with more than five hundred gross of Swarovski crystals—that's 72,000 individual crystals—on one dress. I couldn't take my eyes off this dress. Was this a movie set from Hollywood's Golden Age? I didn't want to leave. I wanted to wear that creation—just once.

"STARS FELL ON ALABAMA," a 1930's song that jazz trombonist and singer Jack Teagarden made famous, refers to the night of November 12, 1833, when a fabulous meteor shower descended across the Southeast. Ever since that celestial event, that night has been known as "the night stars fell on Alabama." This haunting tune ran through my mind as I stood in the middle of Government Street in downtown Mobile, watching its Mardi Gras parade. It was a gorgeous late winter day, the first soft one after a cold snap. It was too early for azaleas, but I saw pink tulips on a white windowsill.

In New Orleans, Mardi Gras is theatrical and pedestrian—it happens in the street and on the sidewalk. Riding on the float in Gulfport was exhilarating, but the crowds in Mobile were the most joyous. It was a multigenerational, multiethnic throng and the joie de vivre was palpable. Elderly couples wearing Mardi Gras beads and sitting on canvas fold-out chairs waited cheerfully for the first parade to come down Broad Street. And there were so many children in our midst.

Just ahead of me, a little boy wearing a gold crown and green Mardi Gras beads was skipping with excitement, barely able to contain himself. He had caught a moon pie! Created around 1917 in Chattanooga, Tennessee, moon pies are the popular "throws" in Mobile. It is a simple pastry, surprisingly tasty (especially when heated). Two graham crackers are filled with marshmallows, covered in chocolate, and shaped big and round like a full moon. Alongside the little boy was a delicate Asian toddler in a pink dress, pink-sequined shoes, and multicolored socks. One black pigtail stood triumphantly on top of her head.

(Imagine a prettier version of the cutest little troll doll you've ever seen, and you'll know exactly what she looked like.) Two red-headed boys, about eleven years old, followed each other on kelly green bicycles tied together by a rope, reminding me of a parade of elephants, each with its trunk wrapped around the tail of the elephant in front of him. The scene made me smile.

The crowd was applauding, whistling, and cheering as the Olympia Brass Band marched by. A vendor selling crazy hats was hawking his wares. A baby nearby, asleep in her stroller, didn't stir.

A white-haired lady, enjoying the scene from her sidewalk chair, offered me a piece of king cake. I was about to decline politely, but the aroma of cinnamon dough was too irresistible, and I enjoyed every morsel.

IF THE PARADES are for the man in the street, the balls are for the aristocracy. The balls draw their customs from the French Bal Masqué and usually celebrate America's European heritage, primarily that of France and Spain. Mardi Gras balls are the exclusive province of krewe members and their guests. It takes a considerable amount of money to be a queen or king of Mardi Gras; I've heard that participants spend between $25,000 and $60,000 for the holiday. They pull out all the stops, preparing a year for the glittering event. Aside from the cost of one's costume, kings and queens entertain their court with a series of lunches and dinners and give them gifts as well.

During the 2003 Mardi Gras season, I was working for the Mississippi Gulf Coast Convention and Visitors Bureau. We invited a visiting journalist from Atlanta to attend a Biloxi Ball. I sat with him as we watched one of the highlights of a tableau ball, the presentation of the court to "royalty." Each member's name was announced as he or she entered. As the court, one by one, solemnly bowed to the royal couple, the writer from Atlanta turned to me. "Are these people serious?" he asked, incredulously.

With the years I've come to realize that this play-acting is another expression of the southerner's sense of beauty, sense of humor, play, and always, a profound love of tradition. It's a source of pride to be the third or fourth generation of the king or queen of Mardi Gras. For a brief time, these community leaders, most of whom work zealously year-round on behalf of charitable organizations, cast off the burdens of work and neighborhood responsibility and indulge in sheer theatrics. You have to embrace the spirit and be willing to suspend your disbelief to appreciate it.

I THINK OFTEN OF RIDING on top of the float and of the man who beseeched me for a trinket. I hope his life has turned out well. What most surprised me as I threw teddy bears, moon pies, beads, and cups to the throng, was that almost without exception, every person who caught a knickknack mouthed the words, "Thank you." And in the midst of this feverish mass of upturned faces, of cries and flailing arms seeking souvenirs, I suddenly saw into the hearts of these people—their struggles, hopes, and joys. I realized that for some people, this was the only party they'd experience all year. And a feeling of intense affection rose up within me—a kinship.

I could never have guessed that I would grow spiritually on top of a Mardi Gras float in Mississippi. But grow I did.

Gym Belles

ONLY ONE OTHER PERSON was working out in the gym when I arrived. . . . Had I walked in on an off-day? Perhaps yet another food festival on the Gulf Coast was keeping people away from their workouts. Was everyone else munching away at a shrimp or crawfish fest or having a barbeque fundraiser? They couldn't be at Our Lady of the Crab Festival; that was last week. Maybe a big bake sale was going on in town. Never mind. Nothing would keep me from doing what I had come there to do.

I had recently moved to Ocean Springs from Manhattan, and I was overjoyed to find a gym only five minutes from our house. Now, I confess that I have never really enjoyed exercising, but I had been in the habit of going to the gym regularly for many years. A good early morning workout at the gym was an essential part of my day. But I soon discovered that

not everyone in south Mississippi shared my commit-
ment to a regular exercise routine. When I was out
having drinks with my new southern girlfriends, I
mentioned that I went to the gym the first thing
every morning. "Good for you!" one of them said
cheerfully, as another chimed in, "Ah should do
that." Then, raising their margarita glasses to their
glossy lips, they picked up the conversation where we
had left off.

I signed up for the only aerobics class offered and
continued working out on the exercise equipment.
After a couple of weeks of being at the gym during
various times of the day, I discovered a number of
local women who made working out a part of their
lives (though by New York and Los Angeles standards, the gym still seemed vacant). But their
approach was different. For one thing, since southerners are such wonderful conversationalists and love
to talk, socializing is a major element of their workout
routine. They even bring their cell phones to class,
and, right in the middle of jumping or pumping, they
actually answer them! They remove themselves from
the group, towel themselves off, and politely retreat
to the back of the room to chat, after which they
rejoin the struggling masses. People in the gym greet
each other enthusiastically and catch up on the latest
news. I watched with amusement (and surprise) as
one woman took her seat on the inner thigh machine

and then spotted a friend, who came over, and the two of them conducted a fifteen-minute conversation. Her companion was perched on the adjacent leg press machine. Neither one of them lifted a leg.

The biggest hurdle I faced in the classes, aside from not understanding the southern drawl over the microphone, was the use of unfamiliar images. In a new step class, the instructor called out the choreography, "Lawn mower!" What the heck was that move? The lawn mowers I had seen cutting the grass in Central Park or around Hollywood houses were riding vehicles that look like small farm implements or maybe very large toys, and a person sat on them. I quickly looked around me at the other women. Without missing a beat, each one jumped onto her step and, using her right arm, reached down to her ankles at an angle and vigorously pulled her arm back to her shoulder; she did this repeatedly. I was perplexed. You can be sure that now I am well-informed that they were mimicking someone trying to start an old-fashioned, walk-behind lawn mower that has a cord you have to pull until its gasoline-powered engine fires.

Of course, I wasn't expecting Mississippi to be L.A., where the cult of the body is paramount. In Los Angeles, there are women who spend several hours every single day at the gym, in intrepid pursuit of the perfect body. Yes, Los Angeles is well known as a plastic surgery center, but it's incorrect to assume Angelinos look so good only because they're on intimate terms with a scalpel. No, indeed! Those women sweat for it. From my fourteen years of living in Southern California, I can honestly say the women I knew tried to eat well; they exercised daily and eschewed smoking; and they knew their vitamin supplements as well as members of their family.

In New York, the attitude towards physical fitness is altogether different. It's efficient. No one has time to spend longer than forty minutes at a workout session. So women whip in and out of high-rise gyms with the same purposeful briskness that they do everything else. Because we all walked at a fast clip in New York, activity was built into the lifestyle. So you didn't panic if you missed your workout one day. After all, you had probably walked to and from the subway and up and down the subway stairs; dashed down the street to a corner supermarket; raced several blocks to a restaurant or department store and the bank during your lunch hour (if you took lunch); and rushed to meet a friend after work for a drink or dinner. New York women work out because they're "heart smart." Of course, they want to be thin because Manhattan is the fashion capital of the country. But for a good part of the year we covered ourselves in layers of clothing: who knew what we were wearing? In Los Angeles, where the weather is pleasant the year around, we dressed in flimsier clothing, so our bodies were always on display.

I've lived in the South twelve years now, and I've seen a distinct change in southerners' attitudes toward physical fitness. People are much more aware today about "getting into shape." That's not to say that they're particularly interested in the subject. When I exit the gym, I often now run into acquaintances. As I chatter away about "low weights and high repetition," I can't help noticing that these ever-polite Mississippians are stifling yawns. As much as southern women may love a good conversation about the vicissitudes of life, believe me, they don't care to discuss the application of exercise theory.

When Mississippi women finally commit to an exercise program, however, they pursue it as vigorously as any New York or Southern California woman. Their energy doesn't flag. One day I questioned a gym mate about her enormous vitality.

"What kind of coffee did you drink this morning?"

"I had what I always have for breakfast—a Coke," she replied.

I was incredulous. "Coca Cola for breakfast?"

"Oh yeah, honey, we like that buzz!"

I'm still astonished at how southern females look when they come to class, even if this is the beauty pageant capital of the world. It's 9:00 a.m. I'm there, bleary-eyed, for step class or maybe it's my

BodyPump group. Before I left home I hastily applied sunscreen, a touch of lip-gloss, and mascara, and I pulled my hair back in a ponytail. Now, I confess, I'm as vain as the next person, and I do want to look nice, but since I know I'll be glowing by the end of the hour anyway, I leave the rest of my ammunition at home. But for many of these women, it's showtime! As we place our mats on the floor, I glance at the young woman to my left. She's wearing a full face of make-up, her hair is completely done, and she has on earrings and a bold 'statement necklace.' When Krystal, our teacher, starts intensifying the pace, I'm concerned that this woman is going to be rolling back up so fast that her jewelry will strike her right in the mouth and knock her front teeth out. So, I keep my eye on her. To my amazement—my awe, in fact—this doesn't happen. And every hair is still in place.

AS THE TWO WOMEN ASTRIDE the inner thigh and leg press machines continued their lively dialogue, I waited patiently to do my daily leg presses, and I worked out on the leg extension machine. Finally, all of a sudden, the women just got up and walked out. They had apparently forgotten why they were there in the first place. I could imagine their answer when husbands or friends asked them what kind of day they'd had. "Oh, it was good—went to the gym and worked out. I'm so glad we finally joined the gym, aren't you, honey?"

As one southern friend once sniffed and said to me, "Ah don't sweat."

Southern belles. You've got to love them.

Southern Wisdom and Wit

AMERICA'S SOUTH HAS PRODUCED some of the most gifted, wisest, and funniest people in our nation. Since I moved to the South, I've collected my favorite quotations, which I offer to you here. Each statement in its own way has enhanced my appreciation of this region. Some make me laugh; others I take to heart. Some days, I pick one and try to live accordingly for the entire day. The following talented southern writers and storytellers are from all over the South: South Atlantic states, Southeast Central states, and Southwest Central states. If you're curious, the place of birth is shown next to each name, followed by the place of greatest association, if different.

H.L. MENCKEN (MD), journalist, essayist:
A cynic is a man who, when he smells flowers, looks around for a coffin.

William Faulkner (MS), novelist, poet:

The past is not dead. In fact, it's not even past.

Tennessee Williams (MS), playwright:

Luxury is the wolf at the door and its fangs are the vanities and conceits germinated by success. When an artist learns this, he knows where the danger is.

Jim Henson (MS), puppeteer:

When I was young, my ambition was to be one of the people who made a difference in this world. My hope still is to leave the world a little bit better for my having been here. It's a wonderful life and I love it.

Katherine Anne Porter (TX), journalist, novelist:

Our being is subject to all the chances of life. There are so many things we are capable of, that we could be or do. The potentialities are so great that we never, any of us, are more than one-fourth fulfilled.

Thomas Wolfe (NC), novelist:

You have reached the pinnacle of success as soon as you become uninterested in money, compliments, or publicity.

Robert Penn Warren (KY), poet, novelist, literary critic:

The poem is a little myth of man's capacity of making life meaningful. And in the end, the poem is not a thing we see—it is, rather, a light by which we may see— and what we see is life.

Thomas Jefferson (VA), third president of the United States, author of the Declaration of Independence:

Determine never to be idle. . . . It is wonderful how much may be done if we are always doing.

Andrew Jackson (SC/NC, TN), seventh president of the United States:

One man with courage makes a majority.

Margaret Mitchell (GA), author:

Until you've lost your reputation, you never realize what a burden it was.

Zora Neale Hurston (AL), writer:

It seems that fighting is a game where everybody is the loser.

Flannery O'Connor (GA), novelist, short story writer:

Whenever I'm asked why southern writers particularly have a penchant for writing about freaks, I say it is because we are still able to recognize one.

Carson McCullers (GA), novelist, short story writer, playwright:

There's nothing that makes you so aware of the improvisation of human existence as a song unfinished. Or an old address book.

Walker Percy (AL), novelist, essayist:

We love those who know the worst of us and don't turn their faces away.

Harper Lee (AL), novelist:

Before I can live with other folks I've got to live with myself. The one thing that doesn't abide by majority rule is a person's conscience.

Truman Capote (LA, AL), novelist, short story writer:

Writing has laws of perspective, of light and shade just as painting does, or music. If you are born knowing them, fine. If not, learn them. Then rearrange the rules to suit yourself.

Failure is the condiment that gives success its flavor.

John Grisham (AR, MS), novelist, short story writer:

Freedom of speech and freedom of expression are so ingrained in our society we rarely stop to think about it. I'm able to write what I want—dark fiendish plots without fear. . . . I can criticize the FBI, the CIA, the president, and Congress without giving it a thought.

Pat Conroy (GA), novelist, memoirist:

Without music, life is a journey through a desert.

My mother, southern to the bone, once told me, "All southern literature can be summed up in these words: 'On the night the hogs ate Willie, Mama died when she heard what Daddy did to sister.'"

Tom Wolfe (VA), author, journalist:

We are now in the Me Decade—seeing the upward roll of the third great religious wave in American history.

Woodrow Wilson (VA), twenty-eighth president of the United States:

America lives in the heart of every man everywhere who wishes to find a region where he will be free to work out his destiny as he chooses.

Lyndon B. Johnson (TX), thirty-sixth president of the United States:

We can draw lessons from the past, but we cannot live in it.

Jimmy Carter (GA), thirty-ninth president of the United States:

War may sometimes be a necessary evil. But no matter how necessary, it is always an evil, never a good. We will not learn how to live together in peace by killing each other's children.

Oprah Winfrey (MS), television host, producer, philanthropist:

Though I am grateful for the blessings of wealth, it hasn't changed who I am. My feet are still on the ground. I'm just wearing better shoes.

Martin Luther King, Jr. (GA), clergyman, civil rights activist:

Our scientific power has outrun our spiritual power. We have guided missiles and misguided men.

Morgan Freeman (TN, MS), actor:

It's sort of well known that anytime any catastrophe happens anywhere in the world, they can count on the United States for help.

Helen Keller (AL), author, activist for the blind and deaf, lecturer:

"Everything has its wonders, even darkness and silence, and I learn whatever state I am in, therein to be content."

Mark Twain (MO), author, philosopher, humorist:

Do something every day that you don't want to do; this is the golden rule for acquiring the habit of doing your duty without pain.

The man who doesn't read good books has no advantage over the man who can't read them.

Robert E. Lee (VA), Confederate Army General, engineer:

A nation which does not remember what it was yesterday does not know where it is today.

Booker T. Washington (VA), educator, orator, author:

There is as much dignity in plowing a field as in writing a poem.

Zig Ziglar (AL, MS), self-help author, religious speaker:

Go as far as you can see and when you get there, you'll always be able to see farther.

Tallulah Bankhead (AL), actress, talk show host:

If you really want to help the American theater, don't be an actress, dahling. Be an audience.

William Ferris (MS), folklorist, historian, southern studies professor:

The American South is a geographical entity, a historical fact, a place in the imagination, and the homeland for an array of Americans who consider themselves southerners. The region is often shrouded in romance and myth, but its realities are as intriguing, as intricate, as its legends.

James Agee (TN), author, journalist, poet, film critic:

God doesn't believe in the easy way.

Jefferson Davis (KY, MS), president of the Confederate States of America:

Never be haughty to the humble or humble to the haughty.

Stonewall Jackson (VA, WV), Confederate general:

You may be whatever you resolve to be.

Eudora Welty (MS), author, photographer:

A good snapshot stops a moment from running away.

A sheltered life can be a daring life as well. For all serious daring starts from within.

Never think you've seen the last of anything.

Through travel I first became aware of the outside world; it was through travel that I found my own introspective way into becoming a part of it.

Patrick Henry (VA), first and sixth governor of Virginia, a founding father of the United States:

I know not what others may choose but, as for me, give me liberty or give me death.

Zelda Fitzgerald (AL), novelist:

We grew up founding our dreams on the infinite promise of American advertising. I still believe that one can learn to play the piano by mail and that mud will give you a perfect complexion.

Fannie Flagg (AL), novelist:

Remember if people talk behind your back, it only means you're two steps ahead!

Jill Conner Browne (MS), author:

Do not ever give a Queen a home appliance as a gift. Period. The end. Now, an exception can be made in the event she just happens to mention in passing that she wishes she had, say, a full Viking kitchen, and then she goes out of town for a few days; and when she comes back, her entire kitchen is renovated with fabulous Viking appliances. She will be touched. On the other hand, if it is her birthday and you, all on your own, select, purchase, and present her with a Crock Pot, well, you are over.

Hank Aaron (AL), baseball player:

I'm hoping someday that some kid, black or white, will hit more home runs than myself. Whoever it is, I'd be pulling for him.

Louis Armstrong (LA), jazz trumpeter:

If you have to ask what jazz is, you'll never know.

Jim Bowie (KY), frontiersman:

*I don't deserve mercy. I do deserve a drink.
You got anything stronger than water?*

Omar Bradley (MO), U.S. Army Five Star General, first Chairman of the Joint Chiefs of Staff:

*If we continue to develop our technology without
wisdom or prudence, our servant may prove to be
our executioner.*

*Ours is a world of nuclear giants and ethical infants.
We know more about war than we know about peace,
more about killing than we know about living.*

*Set your course by the stars, not by the lights
of every passing ship.*

*Wars can be prevented just as surely as they can
be provoked, and we who fail to prevent them, must
share the guilt for the dead.*

D.W. Griffith (KY), film director:

*It takes two years on the stage for an actor or an actress
to learn how to speak correctly and to manage his voice
properly and it takes about ten years to master the subtle
art of being able to hold one's audience.*

W.C. Handy (AL), blues composer and musician:

*Life's something like a trumpet. If you don't put
anything in, you won't get anything out.*

Billy Graham (NC), evangelical Christian preacher:

It is not the body's posture, but the heart's attitude that counts when we pray.

When wealth is lost, nothing is lost; when health is lost, something is lost; when character is lost, all is lost.

Sam Houston (VA, TX), statesman, politician, soldier:

The benefits of education and of useful knowledge, generally diffused through a community, are essential to the preservation of a free government.

Pocahontas (VA), native American princess:

Listen with your heart; you will understand.

James K. Polk (NC, TN), eleventh president of the United States:

No president who performs his duties faithfully and conscientiously can have any leisure.

Will Rogers (OK), humorist, social commentator:

A fool and his money are soon elected.

About all I can say for the United States Senate is that it opens with a prayer and closes with an investigation.

Don't let yesterday use up too much of today.

Even if you're on the right track, you'll get run over if you just sit there.

If advertisers spent the same amount of money on improving their products as they do on advertising, then they wouldn't have to advertise them.

Rosa Parks (AL), civil rights activist:

I have learned over the years that when one's mind is made up, this diminishes fear.

George Washington Carver (MO), inventor, scientist, botanist:

Education is the key to unlock the golden door of freedom.

How far you go in life depends on your being tender with the young, compassionate with the aged, sympathetic with the striving, and tolerant of the weak and strong. Because someday in your life you will have been all of these.

Learn to do common things uncommonly well; we must always keep in mind that anything that helps fill the dinner pail is valuable.

Henry Clay (VA), statesman:

I had rather be right than be president.

Davy Crockett (TN), frontiersman:

Be always sure you are right—then go ahead.

Frederick Douglass (MD), abolitionist:

It is easier to build strong children than to repair broken men.

Willie Morris (MS), writer and editor:

Even across the divide of death, friendship remains, an echo forever in the heart.

Ava Gardner (NC), actress:
Deep down, I'm pretty superficial.

Andrew Johnson (NC, TN), seventeenth president of the United States:
Legislation can neither be wise nor just which seeks the welfare of a single interest at the expense and to the injury of many and varied interests.

William J. Clinton (AR), forty-second president of the United States:
There is nothing wrong with America that cannot be cured by what is right with America.

Frank Hunger (MS), attorney and counselor-at-law.
The difference between hope and despair is a good night's sleep.

Easter 2008

LUCY DENTON WAS SO EXCITED. Two and a half years after Hurricane Katrina, she had just rebuilt on her old home site on the beach in Biloxi. Although the new house wouldn't be furnished yet, we would be "camping out" to celebrate Easter there.

Our core group had always spent the holidays together. The clan this year consisted of Lucy and her twin sons, Jack and Walt; Claire Turner and Delo Burns (friends of the Dentons who're as close as family); Will Denton's old friend Ron Cochran; Walt's wife Courtney and their adorable two-and-a-half-year-old son Turner (they now also have a sweet little girl, Parkes); Jack's girlfriend (now wife) Jean; and my husband Jerry and me. We were disappointed that the Denton daughters, Dawn and Drew, who lived some distance away, couldn't be with us this time. This year, as for the previous three years, Will Denton was not with us. In December 2004, fewer than nine months before Hurricane Katrina devastated the Coast, he had succumbed to a lingering heart condition. But Will's spirit pervaded everything.

JERRY AND I HAD DECIDED not to rebuild on our Ocean Springs property. As lovely as the view of the bayou was, we were hesitant to live on the water again, and the memories of what had been and could never be again made us sad. For us, a fresh start required a different location. Shortly after the storm, Lucy, too, had moved far away from the beach. She bought a gorgeous house in a part of Biloxi that was "high and dry." It was built during the 1970s so, of course, it couldn't have the historic beauty of the home she lost, a 1910 structure with classical architecture and a pediment gable. Still, it was a beautiful place and had an exquisite garden, which Lucy tended carefully.

So I was surprised when, after about a year of living in that new house, Lucy announced her decision to rebuild on the beach. It seemed so risky. Wasn't she happy in the new home, which was in a nice area? "It's not my neighborhood," she said. I was even more astounded when she told us that the new residence she was planning was a modular house. This, from Lucy, who so loved her traditional white columned southern home? She assured me that these factory-built homes were very well constructed. And I knew she was right. In Germany, where anything less than superb construction is unacceptable, modular domiciles have been in use for many years.

But on the day before Easter 2008, Lucy sent an email brimming with disappointment. The house on her old property would not be ready for Easter, so we would go to Claire and Delo's home instead. We understood how badly Lucy wanted to inaugurate her brand-new home on Easter Sunday, but we were still happy to go to Claire and Delo's, knowing that we would all enjoy being together wherever we went. And we did, as people do when they spend holidays with people they've known long and whose friendship they treasure. Of course, the storm had made all of us closer. Poor Ronnie had been ill all week, and none of us would kiss him, afraid of catching the dreaded flu. But he was with us and that was what mattered. After a tasty Easter dinner, Lucy asked Jerry, Ronnie, and me to stop by and look at the new house on her old property.

It was stunning. The view of the beach had a pristine quality I had never seen there before. The air smelled so fresh! Not the salty freshness of an ocean, but a garden-freshness I hadn't smelled on the Coast in a while. But as she took us on a tour and we admired her new residence, I became inexpressibly sad. I remembered her old home, where we had gathered so often. I thought about Will Denton and how his presence was everywhere in the old house. The feeling of loss was overwhelming. Nothing could ever replace that grand old home with the fireplace in the kitchen—one of the coziest eating spots ever. I remembered the marvelous engagement party that the Dentons held a few years ago for their friends Gina and Jonathon, who flew in from New York. We had the most wonderful time on that glorious summer afternoon with Neil, who came in from Hollywood, generously providing Veuve Clicquot Ponsardin for the crowd to celebrate the happy occasion. I remembered the annual Fourth of July parties with masses of people as well as the intimate dinners with just Lucy and Will and Jerry and me at their rustic kitchen table. I tried to hide my melancholia and fought the depression. But I was on the verge of tears. Nothing would ever be the same again.

Just then, when I felt the most miserable, I looked at Lucy as she showed us around her new home. It wasn't just the setting sun that made her eyes glow. For the first time in two and a half years, her finely chiseled face was serene. Clearly, she drew comfort from being back on her old land. The moment reminded me of the scene in *Gone with the Wind*, when Gerald O'Hara admonishes Scarlett: "Do you mean to tell me, Katie Scarlett O'Hara, that Tara, that land doesn't mean anything to you? Why, land is the only thing in the world worth workin' for, worth fightin' for, worth dyin' for, because it's the only thing that lasts. And, to anyone with a drop of Irish blood in them—why, the land they live on is like their mother. . . . It will come to you, this love of the land."

Lucy Conner Denton was back on her land.

It was March 23, 2008. Resurrection.

Acknowledgments

THIS BOOK HAS ITS ORIGINS in my continuing southern experiences, but writing it would not have been possible without the encouragement of my husband Jerry Read. No woman could ask for a more supportive spouse.

I offer my thanks to my editor JoAnne Prichard Morris, for her seamless work and her incisive editorial comments.

Thanks to Barney and Gwen McKee, the publishers of Quail Ridge Press. I'm glad we're working together again.

I'm grateful to Terresa Ray, the managing editor of Quail Ridge Press, whose job title doesn't begin to describe all that she contributes to Quail Ridge's success. I'm especially pleased that she reviews every publication to ensure accuracy.

My thanks, too, to the entire team at Quail Ridge Press for their enthusiasm, particularly Cyndi Clark, whose design and production instincts never fail to produce fine work and who is always available to answer my questions.

Special thanks to my very dear friend and wonderful website designer Renee Palmer. Because of her talents and those of her partners at Pink Rat, LLC, www.daisykaramread.com beautifully reflects my vision of Mississippi.

I owe a debt of gratitude to Walt Denton of Denton Advertising, PLLC, for his excellent guidance on the marketing strategy for this book.

I thank Elizabeth Crisler of Liquid Creative, who helped me with the terrific book cover by attentively listening to my opinions and then sharing her expertise when I was in doubt.

I'm also grateful to my friend and professional organizer, Lita Daniel of Regain Your Space, who transformed my chaotic home office into a serene room, making it possible to write with less stress.